LIFE AIN'T ALL BAD

By Peter Vanden Berg

Eloquent Books
New York, New York

Eloquent Books
An imprint of AEG Publishing Group
845 Third Avenue, 6th Floor - 6016
New York, NY 10022
www.eloquentbooks.com

ISBN 978-1-60693-389-3 1-60693-389-2

Printed in the United States of America

Book Design: Linda W. Rigsbee

Chapters

CHAPTER 1
HOME MOVIES

Some time ago now, my family was together for one of those rare special occasions and for some strange reason we decided to dig into the old movies that my parents kept in the closet. Before long, the ancient 8mm projector was set up and we were enjoying bits and pieces of the hundreds of hours of reel-to-reel tape that my dad had taken through the years. I must confess, I never liked him sticking that old camera in my face on all those family vacations, summer days at the lake, birthdays, or what ever the reason was. But on that particular day, it all seemed to be worth it.

My siblings and I laughed and our kids jeered as the images played out on the wall. You know the images. There were those hideous clothing styles that we all wore and those cat-eye glasses that my mom had when she was hip. My dad stood tall, proud, and vibrant, even while wearing his dark socks and sandals on the shores of Lake Michigan. There was Uncle John and his wife, and what fun they were. Oh look! There was my favorite Aunt Betty preparing her secret pot of spaghetti on a picnic table of some forgotten lake shore. Meanwhile, we kids splashed around in the water. We watched glimpses of our old lab, "Rover," whom I had almost forgotten about, and there was me getting on the school bus for the first day of junior high. My brothers and sisters appeared so young and all of us admitted we looked a bit like oddballs not to mention several pounds lighter. As the reels of tape passed through the ancient projector, we became mesmerized with the past and couldn't stop watching. It was truly a great day.

I drove home that night as my wife and kids slept in the car and couldn't get the movies to stop playing in my head. My Uncle John was strong and stood like a rock in the movies and just last year we buried him. My dad had the same determined look on his face, in the movies, that I often have; yet now dad's face is old and tired. My mom bounced around in the pictures with lots of energy and reminded me of my wife raising our family day to day, yet now mom's so frail and clings to every precious day. Aunt Betty had cancer, and was gone quickly after her role in the movie; and Rover, well, he lived a great dog's life, but it was many years and many dogs ago. I know my brothers and sisters would agree with me that life was really great back then—not a care in the world—and best of all, none of us knew about the struggles and mistakes that lay before us as we would grow up and leave our nest.

I tried sleeping as I lay in bed that night but I knew before long there would be no sleeping. I could not get over the brevity of life and how quickly everything flies by. I wondered if all the "younger" people in the home movies struggled with the same day-to-day stresses that I deal with, and came to the conclusion that they must have. I realized I was currently the same age that Uncle John was in the movies and now he's gone. Aunt Betty was a prime example that life is a gift with no guaranteed end date and I realized how quickly she was here and gone. Most of all, I couldn't shake the overwhelming feeling of how I wanted to be young again and do some things differently this time. I was truly thankful for my parents and cringed when I thought about the times I didn't give my Dad credit and failed to appreciate my Mother's love.

So I made myself a prayerful promise that night, a promise which, in fact, turned out to be the biggest blessing of my life. I promised to find a reason to enjoy every day that the good Lord gives me here on earth and to appreciate the little moments that truly make this life all worthwhile. The best part about the blessing is that it's endless; all I need to do is stop and receive it.

It's the grin that flashes across my son's face when I announce we're off together for an afternoon hunt. It's the sheer pleasure of taking a few moments to enjoy the beauty of my daughter parading around the house in her prom dress, minutes before some lucky young man gets to escort her off for the event. Or, perhaps the look my wife gives me across a crowded room; the look that no one else saw, and that only I know means that she loves me. I now take time some summer nights to sit and watch multitudes of fireflies dance across the open field behind my house and I can't help but wonder if the orchestrated show isn't just for me. There was the day I sat all alone on the snow-topped mountaintop in Idaho and watched an eagle soar over me in all its glory and wonder, and I thanked God for the chance to enjoy His creation. There's the laughter and conversation with the really good friends that I'm lucky enough to have, knowing that my friends unconditionally understand and accept me and that together we'll make it through and be there for each other. Before long, the blessing plays out in so many ways that life becomes a continuous anticipation of wonderful events and every day is a reason to jump out of bed.

However, the blessing isn't a guarantee that life won't have its problems or that tough times won't come. We still bury our Uncle Johns and we all know an Aunt Betty whose life gets cut short. We sadly are forced to put our old dogs down and days spin by when we wonder if we'll ever make it, and sometimes, life just isn't any fun. But the blessing makes for the best home movie one could ever take the time to watch. The blessing is what life should be all about. The show is free and rated G for "great." It's a home movie we all are invited to watch.

CHAPTER 2

SKYDIVING

I went through a period of restlessness when I was thirty-something. I think most guys do. It's not that I was unhappy; I had the basic needs in life—a great wife and three healthy children. Of course, there was never enough money but I didn't starve to death either and the family never went without anything we really needed. I just felt restless, like I needed to do and know more about life.

When I got to work one night, I found an interesting flier hanging on the bulletin board. It was a well-done brochure advertising skydiving for a one day instruction and trial course at a nearby airfield. I instantly snatched the flier off the board and began flipping through the pages, becoming more and more excited as I read it.

"Wow, jumping out of an airplane, how cool," I thought, and began trying to talk some of my fellow comrades into the experience. Most of them looked at me like I was crazy and said "no" but I did get a few takers, more restless thirty-something-year-olds.

Then, as every married man knows, there's the task of talking your wife into it—after all, marriage does mean giving up some freedoms. Of course, I had to be smooth about it; you don't just come home and kick the door open and announce that you're skydiving next Saturday. Gradually, I worked it in that night and got a pretty direct response from her.

"What do you want me and the kids to do when you're dead?" she coldly replied.

I argued on and on and held my ground; this was something I really wanted to check off my bucket list. My wife knew me well enough to know sometimes I'm pretty stubborn about things, so she reluctantly told me to check the life insurance policy and make sure we were covered.

I showed up early that clear September Saturday morning at the airport. The skies were a perfect blue and the sun was creeping up in the East promising a great fall day. I shuffled into the classroom with all the other restless thirty-something-year old men and women and took my seat. They didn't beat around the bush much and handed out a three-page liability release form that undoubtedly, several attorneys had spent a great deal of time on. It was your basic liability form; you promised not to sue the instructor, company, airport, pilots, staff, manufacturers or all the neighbors that lived within three miles of the airport, blah, blah, blah, and they ended by giving some far-out statistic on how many people actually crash.

Not bad, I thought to myself. Then we went through about four hours of classroom instruction, including hanging in harnesses and working through "minor malfunctions" that could occur when you made your jump.

My family showed up about two hours prior to the jump. My wife looked a bit nervous but seemed enthused. A good friend of mine, who is a pilot, also showed up in his plane for the occasion because in his words, he "wanted to see someone dumb enough to jump out of a perfectly good airplane." The stage was set and I walked out onto the tarmac, hoping that the long-haired hippie that packed my chute really knew what he was doing.

I remember heading down the runway wondering just what the heck I had gotten myself into. The instructor asked who wanted to be first and after a short pause from all three of us nervous jumpers, I blurted out "I'll go." My goggles began to completely fog over and my heart pounded so hard I thought I was having the "big one." Sweat was pouring out of every pore and I wondered if I would be able to keep from soiling my pants. We reached the five thousand-foot mark and I was ordered out onto the wing which had two handles that I was to dangle from. I dangled briefly with my legs flopping in the one hundred mile-per-hour breeze and then let go. I remember falling backwards looking at the plane flying away, waiting for what seemed like forever for my chute to open. What followed was the greatest four minutes of my life and to this day I have not been able to replace the feeling. I floated like an eagle and cruised around in the sky, screaming like an idiot. The wind fluttered in my chute and I never wanted to land. The radio set in my helmet crackled with the instructor's voice but I didn't really hear a thing he said. I had a good landing and continued to walk on air. It was a glorious day.

Since that time I've made other jumps. Not any more skydiving jumps—once was enough for me—but other jumps in life. I fully believe that's what God wants us to do in life. So many people never really leave their comfort zone and wonder why they are bored to tears with life. Now I'm not suggesting anything radical like quitting your job, leaving your family and touring the country in a van; there are some limitations. But maybe it's time to stir things up a bit. I know people that won't ever take that special trip with their family because there's not enough time or money. They claim they will do it later. There are people who hate their jobs but are too afraid to take the educated plunge and change careers and enjoy their work once again. Some people go through their marriage as though it's a daily task because they don't want to "jump" and sit down with their spouse and tell him/her they are just not happy and need to work on some change. We are offered so many opportunities in life to be happy but it's up to us to make the change. God never sends a letter in the mail telling us to go ahead with a jump to enrich our lives; he just provides the opportunities. It took my skydiving experience to really drive that point home. I'm glad I did it or I would have missed out on one of the greatest experiences of my life—the experience of jumping.

CHAPTER 3

STEVEN WOOD

'll never forget that afternoon, even though most times I would like to. It was one of those really hot Michigan July afternoons with humidity so thick, you just couldn't get comfortable. I was in the seventh year of my career as a Lansing Police Officer and as I steered my patrol cruiser through the "undesirable" part of town, I could sense it was going to be a long shift.

Not far away, five-year-old Steven Wood was doing what all five-year-olds should be doing on one of those days—playing with his new puppy in the front yard of his home while his uncle and ten-year-old cousin looked on. All of our lives were about to drastically change, even though none of us knew it at the time. I just kept driving my patrol car around, hoping to end the shift without any major incidents and go home in peace.

The toned alert crackled across the radio. Dispatch was receiving numerous calls of a drive-by shooting at an address two blocks from my location. Initial information revealed that two men on a motorcycle pulled up in front of the address and sprayed the house with bullets from an automatic weapon and several people were down. It's the type of call that no matter what you've seen working the streets, you never really get used to this type of violence. I've seen my share of wild things as a street cop but this one was different.

I skidded to a stop in front of the house and jumped out, instantly sensing the unmistakable odor of gun powder that clung to the thick humid air. I confronted the ten-year-old running and screaming around the front yard, who was clinging to his left arm which bore the telltale signs of a gunshot wound. On the front porch steps, I found the uncle, slumped over with bullet holes in his back. A quick check of him and it became apparent he was dead. I ran inside the house and in the foyer was where I found little innocent Steven Wood. He was lying on his back and he looked up at me with his big brown and scared eyes. There was a large hole in his neck and blood was pumping out pretty fast. I knelt down next to him and grabbed his little hand and told him it would be alright—help was on the way. We spent about two minutes together that day—a long, long two minutes. I kept yelling into my radio "how far out are the medics?" and dispatch kept telling me they were on the way. I remember ordering God to save Steven Wood.

"You will *not* let this boy die God; you will not!"

Every time I looked into those big brown eyes, I could tell what he was asking. It was one very simple question—"why?" Steven Wood's precious little life ended that day right there in the foyer of his humble house with me holding onto his little hand telling him it would be alright. I felt the life leave his body just as the ambulance pulled up to the curb.

But there was no time for emotion. I suddenly realized that I hadn't checked the rest of the house for more victims and my training kicked in, causing me to leave Steven lying lifelessly on the floor while I ran through the rest of the house. Just when I thought the agony was done playing out, I observed Steven's father running out the back of the house, loading up his shotgun and screaming with rage and vengeance. He knew who did this and he was off to settle the score. I chased him out into the yard and caught him, tackling him to the ground.

"Don't do it; I can't let you do it," I kept yelling at him while wrestling the gun away from him. More officers arrived on the scene at this point and helped me hold him down until we could get him loaded into a squad car. I returned to the house where several firemen medics were frantically working on little Steven but their faces told the story. It was too late.

I went home that day filled with anger. I was angry at the men who did this; I was angry at the whole situation and how it was probably all about drugs and I was angry at God. My son, who was the same age as Steven Wood at the time, was sleeping in bed when I got home. I peaked in on him and began thanking God for him, but I cut my prayer short.

"Why would you let that happen, Lord?" I said out loud, as I seethed with anger towards God.

For years now, I've thought about that afternoon. There were lots of shootings, lots of violence and lots of agony that I endured during my life as a police officer but that one was different. It was as though I came face to face with true evil and, for the first time in my adult life, my faith was challenged because of it.

None of us really wants to admit there is evil in the world. We often talk about our faith, heaven, and God, and how everything is just fine but we leave out the evil, it is too hard to comprehend. But we should all be aware of evil and in our prayers, include the words from the Lord's Prayer *"deliver us from the evil one".* I know there are two forces in this world— the evil and the good—and some days it seems like the evil is winning. I don't have an answer to the age-old question of why bad things happen. They just do. I believe the devil is hard at work in the world and sin is all around us.

I think that we are all faced with evil at times in our life. Things that make us wonder if God is out there or just too busy to concern Himself with our issues. We find ourselves wondering if the whole notion of good and God even exists and we find ourselves second-guessing our faith.

I've since made my peace with God and through experience and time have learned that life will always have its tragedies, heartaches and sorrows. But you have two choices I figure: you can let evil overcome or you can stand up to it. I know someday evil will be defeated forever and God will destroy it once and for all but until then we are forced to make our choices when we encounter the evil forces that exist. Not all evil is as blatant as what happened to little Steven Wood and it seems to come in all different forms. But when it does, we need to hold our ground, maintain our faith, and believe in our hearts that it will be defeated someday. Until then, stay the course and count your blessings and enjoy the truly good things that can be found in everything that is good in this great ride called "life."

CHAPTER 4

THE PERFECT STORM

I t was a clear and sunny afternoon when I pointed the bow of my twenty-seven-foot Rinker northward on the choppy waters of Lake Michigan that August day. My destination was returning home to my Holland Michigan port after enjoying the day in South Haven with a calculated travel time of one and a half hours. My wife, three kids and I had arrived earlier that day on smooth waters and spent some time with friends and after enjoying the day, it was time to head back.

We were new to boating. We had purchased our vessel earlier that year while shopping for an upgraded camper trailer and discovered our beauty in the parking lot of the used camper store. Although a little cramped, it slept our whole family just fine. It was a dream come true and it offered us a chance to explore the wide open waters of the "the big lake" as we west side Michiganders call it. So we put the camper purchase on hold and decided to try a summer of marina slip rental and boating.

For me it was simple. Look at the clouds, look at the water and set sail for the day. If the weatherman called for severe thunderstorms of course we wouldn't head out but anything short of that, I couldn't miss a chance to be out on the water. I always figured if things got rough, we would just head for shore.

As we watched the pier heads of South Haven disappear that afternoon and got several miles from shore, I sensed something was wrong. The wind seemed to switch directions and the way it hit my face was different. I noticed that the waves began to increase and roll into my bow which at first was a little fun with all that water splashing and parting as my bow slammed through it. Before long, I noticed white caps on the top of the increasing waves and then the big wave hit, causing our boat to jump completely out of the water and slam down before taking on the next big wave. My wife yelled out for me to slow down and head closer to shore, which proved none the better. The sun was gone now and there seemed to be some really dark clouds on the horizon. Before long, things just plain got scary and the waves were now coming up over the boat and drenching me. My wife staggered around the boat and cinched life jackets on the kids and herself saying something like, "I knew we should have stayed in South Haven."

"We'll be fine," I snarled at them, but deep down inside I could feel panic setting in. I could not control the boat anymore and the best I could do was to keep the speeds low and the bow pointed into the waves and let them unleash their fury on us. We were taking on water and still a couple of miles from shore. And the wind—it just wouldn't quit. We were in the perfect storm. I wondered if the bilge pumps could keep up and I too grabbed a life jacket and buckled it snuggly around my neck. Our boat leaped out of the water and slammed down so many times I thought for sure the hull would split wide open. I began eyeing the shore and wondered if we could all swim that far if we capsized, and realized that we couldn't. For some really strange reason, I thought of the words of the song "The Wreck of The Edmond Fitzgerald": *Does anyone know where the love of God goes when the waves turn the minutes to hours?* I began praying earnestly for our safety and desperately longed for the welcoming sight of the pier heads of Holland. For two more hours, we endured the nightmare with my wife and kids crying hysterically and me praying, steering, hoping, and wondering if it would all end OK. Many times I've heard old navy men tell me there are no atheists in a perfect storm and I now know exactly what they mean. After what seemed like five hours, we turned our bow into the channel of Holland and were embraced by the welcoming arms of the piers which turned the boiling and violent seas into semi-smooth water. We limped the boat to our slip and gave thanks to God for bringing us home in one piece. It was a close call and things could have ended much, much worse.

Lake Michigan, I've learned, is a lot like life. It's large and wonderful with lots and lots to explore. It's beautiful and fun to be on and to the inexperienced boater, there never seems to be any danger. But, if you don't research it, respect it, or follow at least some of the basic rules, it will consume you and swallow you up and most times it's too late until you are in the middle of the perfect storm.

Unfortunately, I've gotten myself into the perfect storm on more occasions. Each time, it's the same thing but a different flavor. I start off thinking I've got it under control but a short time later realize the waves are beginning to mount. It's the relationship that starts off good but then big waves crash over it—the little lie I told that needs more fuel to settle the turbulence, the business deal that looked like smooth water but then the water turned into white capped waves. At first it always looks OK, but things can and do change rapidly on the big lake of life.

But I'm learning; I guess that comes with age. I now research the lake forecast a little better, I have a bigger boat, and I don't set sail unless I'm pretty sure of how things are out on the lake. I use radar, depth finders, and have a rubber raft in every business decision, and I realize that God can't always bail me out of poor planning and that there are consequences for my actions. It's hard to enjoy the experience of what the big lake of life has to offer if you're never willing to leave the safety of the pier heads, and exploring the big lake is truly what it's all about. It just takes respect, preparation, and prayer. And when you get to spend the entire day boating on the smooth waters of the big lake of life, you begin to realize, life ain't all bad.

CHAPTER 5
CAMPING

When I woke up in the early morning that day, my air mattress was completely deflated. Every bone in my body hurt, my feet were swollen from sleeping on the uneven ground, my tent was leaking, and I smelled like a combination of the smoky camp fire and burnt paper plates. I was in every sense of the word, not a happy camper.

What is it about camping that makes us want to do it? Lots of people take time off from work, pack up their basic necessities, and flee their busy lives to head for some distant camp ground to "get away from it all." When they get back to reality and their jobs, they stand around and tell others about their camping experience and boast about how they roughed it for the week.

My dad was a camper. For years he insisted that we pack up the wood-sided station wagon and stuff the bulky roof topper with our tent and sleeping bags and head off to some remote place in northern Michigan to go camping. The more remote, the better for him.

"We don't need electricity," he would exclaim, and often-times the bathroom was one of those dreaded places behind that door of the stand-alone building on the outskirts of the property. My job was always to dig the trench around the tent in case we encountered the torrential downpours that can occur in the summer months of northern Michigan. From an early age, I learned that water always ran to the lowest place, it only takes one time to have all your belongings completely soaked to drive that point home. When I got married, my wife and I bought our first pop-up camper and proudly set it up in the yard, waiting in great anticipation to head off to the Yogi Bear Campground and stake our own claim as campers. And so it went for years, and now I often wonder if my kids will continue the tradition and label themselves as "campers."

There are great stories that come out of camping—stories that are fun to tell when sitting around other campfires, at parties, or during an evening with friends. Just about any experienced camper will tell you of the time when….which is usually one of the most hilarious experiences they can remember as a time together with family or friends. The campfire is also a magical place where stories are told, laughter is abundant, and the "smores" never tasted better. There doesn't seem to be a need to worry about clean feet or combed hair around the campfire. After all, "we're camping." Adults drink from Styrofoam cups and reminisce out loud, oftentimes revealing far too much information to the others around the fire, while the kids run around without worry, catching fireflies or playing Darth Vader games with flash lights in the dark.

I've pondered that for some time now and can't help but wonder if that isn't just what camping is all about—a remote and relaxed needed time out with friends and family. After all, it can't be because you enjoy waiting in line to use the bathroom and shower or because you appreciate constantly chasing flies off your gourmet meal that you've cooked over an open fire with ashes stuck to your burger.

The days of getting together seem to be far and few between and I can't really say it's any better or worse than it used to be. People have always been busy and found reasons to not do things together, but deep down inside, all of us we really want to take time out with each other. Camping forces us to be together. Brothers sleep next to their sisters (yuck), husbands and wives share the same air mattress or crowded sleeping area only several feet away from the kids, and eating meals may happen around some fold-out table that causes us to invade each other's comfort level. I'm often disappointed when I hear someone say that their idea of the perfect camping trip is checking into the local upscale hotel for the week; it just seems like they're missing the point.

We rush around in life and sometimes it's easier to sit in the comforts of our homes, clicking the remote in air-conditioned relaxation than it is to hunker down under some hot canvas enclosure and call it a vacation. But, if you find a family that's spent time camping, you will also find a family that's close and genuinely loves each other. They have taken the time to be together as a unit. They really know each other and what the personality traits are of one another. They know what it's like when the wind blows or what a true thunder storm is. Kids know the meaning of the summer campground romance and adults can relate to laughing so hard that their sides hurt the next day. A family is a fragile unit, easily broken and sometimes not a smooth operation, but camping seems like the ultimate Band Aid for placing it all back into perspective. Friendships are strengthened after camping trips, and life slows down enough for us to enjoy the small stuff.

Summers come and go just like the rest of our seasons. Perhaps this summer it's time for all of us to consider a time out with the ones who really make this life what it should be—an incredible journey.

CHAPTER 6

MR. JOHN

I grew up on the outskirts of a small nowhere town on the southwest end of the greater Grand Rapids, Michigan area. We lived in a humble home two houses west of a major highway with an exit to our road. It was not unusual for us to experience a knock at the door at all hours of the night and find a stranded motorist standing there asking for help or to use the phone. After all, it wasn't like they could call for help from their cell phones.

I was about eleven years old when I got home from school one spring day. My mother was speaking to a very large and odd looking man in our driveway when I got off the school bus and I figured he was just another highway stray. When I walked up to them, I could sense the man mom was talking to was not what I considered normal. He towered over both of us and was quite sunburned over most of his sunken-in face. His speech was slow and deliberate and I quickly learned from the conversation that he didn't know his last name, didn't know where he was from, and didn't know where he was going. His clothes were torn and very dirty and he smelled awful. About all he could tell us was that his name was John and that he had not eaten in quite some time. But there was one unmistakable character trait to him—his eyes. I'll never forget those eyes. They were the most crystal blue I had ever seen and when he looked at you, it was almost like he looked right into your soul.

Mom took Mr. John into the breezeway area of our home and ran into the kitchen to make him a sandwich while I stared in awkward silence at the mysterious giant seated on our wooden bench. While Mr. John munched on his sandwich, mom called the local sheriff department and explained the peculiar situation to the dispatcher who reluctantly sent out a deputy sheriff. I remember the deputy searching Mr. John and asking for ID and after learning nothing about our stranger, he told my mom there was very little he could offer for the man and left. Mom wouldn't give up and called my Uncle John, who also had a large physical frame, and explained the situation, stating she needed some clean clothes for our new guest. My dad arrived home from work later on and took Mr. John down to the basement and offered him a shower in the basement bath. That night we all sat down for dinner and watched Mr. John consume large portions of one of my least favorite cabbage dinners. Mom fixed up a cot that night and offered Mr. John a bed in our breezeway and before long he was sleeping soundly while mom and dad talked over what to do with our mystery stranger.

The next day, I returned home from school and found Mr. John tilling up our large country garden with a spade shovel. My mother, like any good Hollander, figured if he was going to stick around and eat he might as well pitch in and do some work, so she steered him out to our garden with the shovel. I then took an instant shine to Mr. John since he basically eliminated the back-breaking work that loomed before my brother and me that coming Saturday. So I wandered out to the garden and began speaking to Mr. John. I did most of the talking; he just stared at me with those mysterious blue eyes.

A week or so passed by as Mr. John became a regular at our house. My mother would read the Bible to him in the evenings after dinner and we would all try to learn more about him—

where he was from, where he had been, and what plans he had—but we never really seemed to get any helpful information. I enjoyed spending time with Mr. John; he was easy to talk to and seemed genuinely interested in the issues of my eleven-year-old life. Every night, Mr. John would tuck himself into his cot and sleep soundly until the next morning when he would awake, eat, and do some more chores. My parents grew fond of Mr. John as my dad worked a lot of hours and appreciated the extra help around the house.

When I woke up the following Saturday and heard my mother talking to Mr. John in the driveway, it was very apparent he was leaving. He simply announced it was time for him to go, and had his basic things packed together and began walking down the road. I ran downstairs into my bedroom and frantically looked around for something to give him as a parting gift. The only thing I could find was my brand new red and tiny Gideon Bible that I recently received at school, so I snatched it up and ran upstairs to find my bicycle in the garage. I peddled up to Mr. John as he was nearing the entrance ramp for the highway and yelled out, "Mr. John, wait, I have something for you!" He smiled when I handed him the little book and he paused for a moment to fan through the pages of his tiny treasure. He then looked at me with those deep blue eyes and simply said, "Thank you, Peter." I drove away from him with tears in my eyes, and realized how fond I had become of him. A short ways down the road, I stopped my bike and looked back. Mr. John was gone.

I've thought about Mr. John from time to time during my life. I have no idea what happened to him and to this day he remains a mystery to our family. I don't know why I gave him a Bible—I was not in any way a young evangelist—it just seemed like the right thing to do at the time. It wasn't until later on in life when I think I found the answer to this mystery. It was during a low point in my life when I felt the need to really search the Bible for some answers to some tough questions I had when I found a verse in Hebrews 13:2 that made me think of Mr. John. *"Don't forget to be kind to strangers, for some who have done this have entertained angels without realizing it!"*

My thoughts turned to Mr. John and I wondered if he was an angel. I know it sounds a little far fetched but I just couldn't forget the eyes. His eyes were kind and understanding, almost as if he knew me. My mother always told me that the eyes are a mirror of the soul and I suppose some day I'll know the answer to the whole mystery. I'm thankful for parents who taught me the reality of living that Bible verse.

We all meet strangers in our life and it's a little uncomfortable to think about what we've said to them or how we have treated them. I'm not sure God sends angels that taunt us or try to deceive us but I believe we are all tested from time to time. Actions always speak so much louder than words and actions to strangers are really a true test of our character. It's what we do and say to them, when no one else is watching, that truly reflects on who we are. I firmly believe we should never "judge a book by its cover" when it comes to the people that we meet in life. It's hard not to judge strangers and I'm guilty of it all the time, but we are called to love our neighbors/strangers as ourselves. There are lots of opportunities to help strangers and by doing so, we can all enrich our lives in the great ride of life. And who knows, we just might be entertaining angels.

CHAPTER 7

HOPE

I t was another night of driving the patrol car around the streets. I was working what we called "the special shift"—8 p.m. to 4 a.m.—the shift with all the action—the shift that was perfect for the restless one.

The call came in about 2 a.m. of a possible arson; neighbors were reporting a car on fire in the street. I arrived within minutes and noticed that the car wasn't in the street; it had in fact crashed into a tree on the side of the street and was fully engulfed in flames. Cautiously, I walked up to the car and when I reached the driver's door, I saw her. The driver was still inside and pinned behind the steering wheel and could not escape the flames that had burned her legs, burned her body, and were beginning to burn her face. Her screams were muffled by the roar of the flames and she was using her right hand to bat at the intensely hot and increasing bright orange flames consuming her. I ran back to my patrol car and found a fire extinguisher in the trunk and raced back to the burning car to help. I remember spraying the extinguisher on her face and pulling on her left hand, pulling off only burnt skin, and unable to remove her body from the wreckage. Another officer arrived and he too used his extinguisher and helped me pull on the now unconscious driver. With the help of a pry bar from a neighbor, we freed her foot and dragged her charred body out of the car into a snow bank. The arriving paramedics placed her on a back board and loaded her into the waiting ambulance.

"She'll probably be dead when we get there," one of them told me, and raced away for the hospital while remaining firemen extinguished the burning vehicle.

When I returned to my patrol car and climbed in, I realized I was shaking pretty bad. The terrible smell of burnt flesh clung to my nose cavities and try as I might, I couldn't blow the smell out. My eyes stung from the smoke and flames and my uniform appeared charred in places. I attempted to wash off the burnt skin that stuck to my hand in a nearby snow bank and although gone, it continued to send shivers up my spine. There had been plenty of gory accidents that I had witnessed up to that point but never before had I watched fire engulf a human being.

Next came the investigation; why had the car left the street, who was the driver, and what was the cause of it all? The roadway was fairly clear and there were no skid marks on the pavement. No other cars were in the area and something just didn't seem to fit. The driver was now at the hospital and amazingly, she was conscious and talking to the doctors. She relayed one important comment as hospital staff pumped her full of morphine—she screamed out that she had tried to kill herself by slamming her car into the tree and was pleading with the doctors, to just let her die.

A few days passed and miraculously, she continued to live. I learned that her first name was Hope. "Kind of bitter irony" I thought to myself, since that's what she gave up. Investigation revealed that Hope had been a victim of sexual abuse from a family member for many years and the day of Hope's crash was ironically the anniversary of her mother's death a year earlier—also a suicide. Hope was a younger girl with her whole life in front of her but things were too overwhelming early on in her life and she had simply given up.

Hope became one of the lucky ones. After months of surgeries and physical rehab, she was released from the hospital and returned home. I don't know what happened to her after that. There were many suicide attempts that didn't turn out so good on my shifts as a street cop. Suicide is one of those statistics that no one really likes to keep track of but that I can assure you, is all too common. Suicide calls always depressed me. It's such a permanent solution for what most times, were temporary problems. Young and old, they gave up hope because life became too much to handle. Families were always left with complete shock and loved ones were forced to pick up the pieces and continue on. The harsh reality of suicide is that help was just too late—the decision was final and irreversible and all hope was lost.

Giving up hope is a feeling that I know everyone goes through from time to time. There's the spouse that left, the lost career, the addiction we can't shake, bills that never go away, the agony of failure, and happiness becomes a distant memory. For guys my age it seems, sometimes, as though we go to work, pay the bills, and get up and do it all over again the next day, with no end in sight, no appreciation, and so very, very routine. We're human and although we expect ourselves to be perfect, we realize we're not. We make some really bad choices in life and want "do overs" only to realize that there are none. We sit in church and wonder how *that person* always seems to be so happy and have it all. We wish our family was like the family down the road and little by little we begin to give up hope.

I wonder what God thinks when we give up hope. He created us, gave us our whole life to live, choices to make, and some basic rules to follow for a recipe of happiness. Yet we sometimes seem to mess it all up and spiral down, giving up hope. We are told early on by Sunday school teachers and ministers that God loves us and to be thankful for our blessings and to spend time in prayer, but it's easy to scoff off the notions and think our situation is different and really bad.

Giving up hope is really depression. Depression can be fatal if not treated and if you think you may have a developing problem with depression, please get professional help. But I think that mild forms of depression that we all encounter come from what we pile on ourselves. In today's world it seems too many of us are always trying to "keep up with the Joneses" and we look at the grass on the other side of the fence, thinking it's greener over there. So we work more hours to buy the things that Mr. and Mrs. Jones have and we jump over the fence, forgetting to water our own grass a little more, only to find out we become more exhausted and more depressed to balance it all.

Is your glass half full or half empty? I always say, what does it matter— fill up your glass again! When was the last time you honestly sat down with a piece of paper and wrote out the blessings that you have? How long has it been since you took the time to watch a sunset, or really talked to your kids, or stayed home long enough to appreciate the roof over your head and the many things under that roof? What about all those payments—do you really need the stuff or would it probably be better to sell it off and shed the debt? The bad crash that left damage can heal, but it will first need some attention to address the problem that caused the crash. God wants us to be happy and to ask him for our daily basic needs, but it's up to us to take time and enjoy the things we're given instead of wanting more. Life is a great gift and we can't make it any better by adding more stuff, comparing ourselves to others, or strapping ourselves with stress. Wake up tomorrow and force yourself to find a reason to enjoy each day with what you've been given. You just might be surprised to find that life ain't all bad.

CHAPTER 8

GIVING

I t was in the spring of 2001 when I decided to leave my career as a policeman. I was bored to death with the job. The administration seemed to have distanced itself even further from the reality of it all. I was tired of making domestic disturbance calls and fighting with drunks, and I grew hard from observing the senseless nightly violence and tragedies. I was dead inside.

I had been involved in construction while working at the police department for quite some time, building houses in the morning and patrolling the streets at night. Day after day I longed for the chance to build homes on a full time basis, and when I reached the fifteen year mark at the police department and vested my pension, I decided to "jump" and give it a try. It offered the chance to make more money, be independent, and be home on Christmas once in a while. I knew I needed to be a better father, husband, and person and it just didn't seem possible to continue on as I had been, trying to balance it all.

Construction went well, my attitude got better, and my life definitely improved. I must shamefully admit though, I wasn't much of a giver back then. I had worked jobs since I was twelve years old and I counted every dime. The thought of true giving was always replaced by the thought of the kids needing new shoes for school, the overdue bills that sat on my desk, or the next toy that I had on the wish list.

I soon realized that life as a builder had its ups and downs like any other job, and for builders, the job is kind of a gamble. You go to the bank and borrow the money, build your idea of the perfect home, and then sit back and wait for a buyer. The longer the house sits, the more your profit disappears. The bank wants their interest payments, the tax man wants his cut, and you still have to pay the heat and light bill. If the home reaches the dreaded "birthday," meaning the one-year mark with no buyer, profits are pretty much gone and you begin to go upside down on the investment. I had one such home sitting in a development that I took a gamble on. The birthday was looming in the near future, and we were about to go upside down on it.

My wife came into my office that day while I anxiously reviewed the books on the project and told me the bad news. Our neighbor had unexpectedly passed away, leaving his wife all to herself and the neighborhood was taking up a collection to help with expenses. I knew the neighbors didn't have much and money was tight for them and, having been causally inspired by a recent sermon my preacher gave on giving, I decided to write out a check. I surprised myself somewhat when I filled in the amount and felt gracious about myself. I still remember writing out the last part of my name on the check when the phone rang. It was an offer on the house I had for sale and—long story short—I sold it. I remember thinking at the time that maybe it was a result of giving, but I soon wrote it off as a house that was "bound to sell" since it neared the birthday mark.

Sunday came and I felt the need to drop a little extra in the collection plate—after all I had just made a sale. Later that week, the phone rang again and much to my surprise, I signed up another custom build job with a guaranteed paycheck upon completion. So I decided to give a little more and the next week it happened again, more work. It happened again and again and looking back on it all now, I believe it was the beginning of a giving-maturing process unfolding for me.

There's a verse in the Bible—Luke 6.38—that we all hear about quite often. *"For if you give, you will get! Your gift will return to you in full and overflowing measure, pressed down, shaken together to make room for more, and running over. What ever measure you use to give—large or small—will be measured what is given back to you."* I must admit, I'm quite turned off by religious institutions that dangle that verse on the bottom of their letters that I receive in my mailbox in November as they ask for money to meet their yearly expenses. They turn a great verse into sounding like a hollow religious casino promise: "give to us and you will get rich." I don't mean to undermine that Bible verse—it is in fact the gospel truth which I have experienced over and over—but I think there's more we need to understand about giving. True giving comes from your heart. It's an exercise in giving back a portion of what you have been blessed with and having faith to know you will receive more. You begin to understand that you really didn't make the money; God gave it to you and we are expected to give something back. I don't like percentages either. Many people reluctantly give a fixed percentage of their income to their churches and call themselves givers. I think we should give portions, portions of what we have to really illustrate that we are thankful for our blessings and often times realize it's more that "x percent."

We all have a chance to give. If you know of someone who is struggling to put groceries on the table for the family, drop off a bag. No need to leave your name, God knows you did it. There are people who don't give because they say they have no extra money. What about your time? Perhaps you can give by simply taking time to listen to someone who needs to talk over some problems in their life. What about taking that precious Saturday morning that we all cherish, and helping out someone in need with their projects or chores. Don't worry about the payback, God keeps track and will reward you. Don't give thinking that Ed McMahon will ring your doorbell tomorrow and announce that you won the Publishers Clearing House Sweepstakes; it doesn't work like that. Your self righteous contribution in the collection plate on Sunday won't result in holding the lucky winning lottery ticket that following Friday. Give because you can and watch out for the awesome results!

Over time now I've been blessed with the realization of what it means to be a true giver even though I stumble often. I continue to be blessed with work even though it may not be the amount that I always want. Giving brings a peace to my life, and I've begun to realize that I will always have what I need as I continue on in this day to day journey.

CHAPTER 9

SLIPPERY

Chances are you remember exactly where you were and what you were doing when you first heard the news of September 11. It was one of those moments in life that happen every so often, moments that force us to put aside our daily routines and face a harsh reality of this world.

I had one of those moments a few years ago, and I remember exactly what I was doing when I got the call that January day. "Slippery has cancer and it does not look good," a friend of mine shared with me. My mind whirled at first and then I tried to reason the situation a little bit. How could it be, he's only in his forties! "What about chemo, radiation, or all the other methods?" I asked. After all, these are modern times! The answer I received was pretty depressing. Small cell cancer had a very low recovery rate and with a good fight it would maybe buy Slippery six months to live.

Slippery was my marina neighbor who we lived next to on the summer weekends after spending the days floating on the waters of Lake Michigan in our boat. He and his wife, Lynn, were in the prime of their lives and shared a beautiful vessel named *The Slippery Lynn* which they took great pride in owning, waxing, and detailing to perfection every chance they got. Slippery's real name was Steve and he was a unique individual, right down to his nick name, Slippery. Slippery took my family under his wing from early on in our boating adventures and never refused to offer us information and assistance as we were rookies at boating. Slippery was an old hat at sailing and I hung on to every word and piece of advice he offered. If we had a malfunction with our boat, he was one of the first to help out, and took simple pleasure in offering his tools, advice, and knowledge anytime I asked. As time passed, I took a fond liking to Slippery and oftentimes we would sit on the docks until early in the morning sharing stories, laughing, and enjoying libations. He was truly a great man.

I knew I had to call Slippery when I heard the news but my hands shook when I picked up the phone. What do you say to a man who's been handed a death sentence?

"How's it going, Slip?" I managed to get out when he answered. I was surprised by the tone in his voice; it was confident and assuring as he told me he had a "hiccup" and that he planned on a good fight with some new medications and trend-setting techniques. Several months passed and the reports that came in were not good. As boating season came upon us that spring, I again spent time at the marina with my neighbor and watched him daily decline in health. As the summer progressed, Steve lost muscle strength and the cancer ate away at his body until he was too weak to walk anymore. Steve's lifelong wish was to take his *Slippery Lynn* up to the North Channel of the Great Lakes—something he planned to do when he retired, when there would be more time and money. Since we all knew he would never see that day, some of us planned a boat trip up to Pentwater for the weekend, a last hurrah for Steve and his boat. I remember sitting in the port that weekend, each one of us taking some one-on-one time with Steve to say our last goodbyes. When my turn came, I didn't know what to say. After some chit chat, I worked up the courage and asked Steve if he had things square with God and he assured me he did. I remember him painfully telling me he just wished he had more time to enjoy his family, friends and life, and that he didn't understand why God cut him short.

As summer came to an end, so did Slippery's life and he went home to his Lord and Savior late that August. The funeral was a celebration of his life and we sprinkled his ashes in the choppy waters of Lake Michigan. I sat in the marina after the funeral all alone, and watched his boat bob up and down while tied to the dock. It seemed like only yesterday Steve was on the bow, washing and scrubbing and yelling out at me about the size of the waves on the big lake. I thought about how quickly it had all gone and I began to remember some of the classy things Slippery did prior to his death. Early that summer, Steve took the time to walk his daughter down the church aisle for the someday wedding that he would have to miss. As painful as it was, he took the opportunity to say goodbye to all his friends and family and even took time to plan the care of his boat for the upcoming winter. I remembered the last time we ate dinner together on the picnic table of the marina and the look on his face as he looked across the open water. Most of all, I remembered what he said to me that day in Pentwater about wanting more time—more time to enjoy what mattered the most—his family and friends.

Since Slippery's death I've thought a lot about my own death. Death and dying is something that none of us likes to talk about, especially those of us in the prime of our lives. Each one of us knows that death is coming, yet it's too hard to dwell on now. "Wait until we're older," we subconsciously say. We often wonder how we will meet the end and I think most of us want to die peacefully in our sleep after we've reached the mental and physical capacity of our lives. The reality of it all is that life is so very, very short. Our lives are nothing more than a dot on an endless line of eternity and none of us are guaranteed a death on our schedule. Solomon said it best in the Bible book of

Ecclesiastes 11.7-8: *"It's a wonderful thing to be alive, if a person lives to be very old, let him rejoice in every day of life, but let him also remember that eternity is far longer, and that everything down here is futile in comparison."*

I now try to live my life here on Earth with the words Slippery left me, using the precious time that I have. Time is something that we never get back and although it seems to drag some days and zoom by other days, it clicks away at the same pace as it did yesterday, today, and tomorrow. I've learned in the short time I've been alive that there may not be a tomorrow and now I try to appreciate every detail of life today. There are obligations in life, of course, and we can't shirk those in the name of time and live life like it's over tonight. However, I think we all need to live a little bit more consciously of our time. Some of the things we think are so important now just don't seem to matter several years down the road and when we look back, we wonder why we worried so much about them. If we're truly honest, most of our good memories involve our family or friends—the same people that help us through the bad times. Yet oftentimes we seem too busy to spend a few moments with the ones that matter because we are off chasing other priorities like money, careers, and false comforts.

So today is another day for you with more sweet precious time. Only you can decide on how to use the time and in the end, won't it be great to face God and thank him for the great gift that he gave us—the gift of life.

CHAPTER 10
DO OVERS

'**ve had a dog for as long as I can remember. They offer just too much love to turn down, I guess. I often think that dogs know us better than anyone else; they can sense our moods and respond silently. The thing about dogs that always intrigues me is that I wonder what they would say if they could talk. That thought is usually and quickly replaced with the thought that I'm glad they can't talk.

The weekend started out like any other weekend—errands to run, a small punch list stuck to the fridge, time to mow the lawn, the usual mid-life routine weekend stuff. I pulled out of the driveway early that Saturday with two of my three kids in my pickup truck, heading off to begin the day. About a hundred yards down the road I looked in my rear-view mirror and saw our one-year-old overly ambitious Jack Russell Terrier running down the road, trying to catch up to the truck. We had been trying to break our new puppy into staying in the yard but the dog had way too much energy and it was becoming a challenge. I reluctantly pulled over and let her in. After all we shared one thing in common—neither one of us ever wanted to miss out on an adventure.

Our first stop was at a friend's house on a busy road. I told the kids to wait in the truck while I ran in to drop off some paper work. About three minutes into the conversation, my son came crashing through the door screaming, "she's been hit!" My heart sank and I ran out the door at top speed only to see my daughter sobbing uncontrollably and hunched over our lifeless dog in the ditch next to the road. The kids had accidentally opened the door to the truck and our dog jumped out and raced across the busy street to join company with the neighbor's dog only to be struck by an oncoming car. To make matters worse, the driver sped off after the crash, leaving my kids all alone with the injured animal. I scooped up the dog and placed her in the truck and sped off to the vet's office only a mile away. We bolted through the door and the expression on our faces told the staff exactly what happened. I telephoned my wife and told her what had transpired and she and my youngest daughter arrived in minutes while my other two kids were on their knees praying earnestly in the lobby of the vet's office for God to save our dog. For those of you who have gone through this, you know it's one of the worst days of your life, it's like losing a family member.

The five of us circled the lifeless dog on the table and heard the vet say the dog's heart was barely beating and perhaps we could transport her to the emergency room at Michigan State University and work on her. The thought of the bill that came with an emergency medevac transport to an animal emergency room sent chills up my spine so I asked the vet to do the humane thing and hasten the inevitable and give her "the shot". I nodded one last time at the vet while holding back tears from watching the misery on the faces of my kids.

On the drive home we were all silent, sad, and heartbroken. We had a small Styrofoam coffin in the back seat and my weekend list now included conducting a burial in the backyard. I still remember the look on my kid's faces, dealing with the harsh reality of it all. When I asked my youngest daughter how she was doing she looked at me and simply said, "I wish we could start this day over, daddy." I was crushed, realizing this was probably the first time in her life that she wanted a do-over, the first moment in her life when she realized what most of us know—that life can be brutal sometimes and we just want the chance to start over.

There's not a person alive who hasn't wanted a do-over. Some times it's casual and sometimes there's a desperate agonizing longing for the chance to start over. "We've all done things that we're not proud of," an old salt on the police department used to tell me and isn't that the truth? Things seem to go from OK to really bad sometimes and we say to ourselves that if given the chance, we would do it right this time, do it differently. I don't need to fill in the blanks here with examples. Everyone has a story.

Famous Beatles singer, Paul McCartney, knew the pain of do-overs which he sang about in his song, "Yesterday."

"Yesterday, all my troubles seemed so far away, now it looks as though they're here to stay, oh I believe in yesterday."

The reality of it all, of course, is that there aren't any do-overs. We are stuck with the past, the things we did and said, and the decisions we made. To wish for a chance to do-over is a waste of time; it doesn't happen. We can, and did, buy another dog but the old dog was gone forever and although we were thankful for the time we had with her, it didn't change the facts.

Now I don't have the perfect recipe to combat longing for yesterday but the only chance I see to replace the nagging feeling of wanting a do-over is through forgiveness. Forgive yourself, forgive others, and move on. Forgiveness is really tough; in fact it's the hardest thing for me. Some of us are Mr. and Mrs. Relentless. "You made the choice, you suffer through it," we say. And it's true, we must sleep in our own beds that we created but to constantly beat yourself up never gives you the chance to forgive yourself or others. God created us as human beings and try as we might, we will fail, mess up, and wish we could do it over from time to time. Forgiving doesn't necessarily mean you have to forget; after all, we don't want to make the same mistakes again. But forgiving gives us a fresh start, a chance to do some things differently next time. Fresh starts are what keep us going, they breathe life into us and season us to handle the challenges that we face every day. Forgiving is the ultimate act of love.

God forgave you; can you step up and forgive yourself or others? Drop the heavy back pack of guilt and give it a try, a chance to live life free from the wish of a do-over.

CHAPTER 11

CONCLUSION

And so our time together comes to an end, like all things do in life. My hope is that I connected with someone, a person like me, somebody very average, and just like you. Our connection identifies us. We're caught somewhere between the excitement and inexperience of youth and the wisdom and brevity of old age. We are moms and dads, children, friends, and neighbors all traveling through this journey together. Life is not always a fun ride and we sometimes lose hope and want do-overs. We are expected to have all the answers, solutions, and time; yet we fail often. I think we all know that God is in control. It just seems a little scary some days and we wonder if God is just too busy for us. At times, our faith begins to fade when evil stares us in the face. We make mistakes and bad choices all the time and realize that all we can do is try better tomorrow. We are people finding our way through life, still in training.

There are many people who have the burning ambition to find out why they are here on this Earth; they want a clear purpose for their life. I can't help but wonder if we don't sometimes miss the whole point and need to realize that maybe our purpose is simply to enjoy this life that God has given to us. Enjoyment that comes from the everyday things of life, not just the big goals or accomplishments. Enriching our lives with the people and strangers around us, regardless of their beliefs and issues we may think they have. The gift of nature and all its glory. Giving freely of our gifts of money and time and receiving more in return. Forgiveness and fresh starts. Jumping and discovering the big lake of life. All of the wonderful things that are handed to us every day, if we just take the time to appreciate them.

There are many more stories but we'll save those for another day, I suppose. My prayer is that you will receive many more years to enjoy your journey and that you will receive the same great blessing that I have. The blessing of life.

Printed in the United States
142258LV00001B